Frugal Frenzy

A Guide to Living Lavishly on a Lean Budget

The Art of Frugal Living

Welcome, my friends, to the wonderful world of frugal living! If you're reading this book, chances are you're ready to take control of your finances and start living life on your own terms. And let me tell you, there's no better way to do that than by embracing the art of frugalism.

Now, before we dive in, let's get one thing straight. Frugal living isn't about depriving yourself or living a life of misery. It's about finding smart, creative ways to save money so you can have more of it to spend on the things that really matter to you. It's about living life to the fullest without breaking the bank.

Think about it: when you're spending less on the little things, you're freeing up more of your hard-earned cash for the big stuff. Whether it's traveling the world, starting a business, or simply having more financial security, frugal living can help you get there.

And the best part? Frugal living is accessible to everyone, regardless of income. Whether you're living paycheck to paycheck or making six figures, the principles of frugalism can be applied to your life.

So, buckle up and get ready to take control of your finances. This book will be your guide to frugal living, teaching you everything from how to budget effectively to how to have fun without spending a fortune. We'll cover it all, and we'll have a blast doing it.

Now, let's get started!

Mindset Matters: Shifting Your Perspective on Money

Ladies and gentlemen, it's time to get real. The truth is, your relationship with money starts in your head. If you want to be successful with frugal living, you need to shift your perspective on money and start thinking differently.

First things first, let's bust a myth. Frugal living isn't about being cheap or lacking in generosity. It's about being mindful with your money and spending it wisely. When you have a frugal mindset, you appreciate the value of a dollar and make conscious decisions about how you spend your hard-earned cash.

So, how do you shift your perspective on money? Start by getting real about your financial situation. Write down your income and expenses and take a good hard look at your spending habits. This will give you a clear understanding of where your money is going and help you identify areas where you can cut back.

Next, get rid of the "keeping up with the Joneses" mentality. We live in a world where we're constantly bombarded with messages telling us we need more, bigger, and better. But the truth is, more isn't always better. By embracing a frugal mindset, you'll learn to focus on what's truly important in your life and stop comparing yourself to others.

Another key aspect of a frugal mindset is being proactive. Instead of waiting for opportunities to fall in your lap, you take the bull by the horns and create your own opportunities. This means finding ways to earn extra income, negotiating bills and prices, and finding smart ways to save money.

Finally, remember that frugal living is a journey, not a destination. Don't get discouraged if you slip up and spend too much money on something. The important thing is to learn from your mistakes and keep moving forward.

So, are you ready to shift your perspective on money? Let's get started! The road to frugal living starts with a change in mindset, and with the right attitude, you'll be well on your way to financial freedom.

The Power of a Budget: Tracking Your Spending

Listen up, folks! If you want to be a frugal living pro, you need to master the art of budgeting. And let me tell you, a budget is your secret weapon to taking control of your finances.

First things first, let's define what a budget is. Simply put, a budget is a plan for how you're going to spend your money. It helps you keep track of your income and expenses and ensures that you're living within your means.

Now, I know what you're thinking. "Budgeting sounds boring and time-consuming." But trust me, once you get the hang of it, budgeting can be fun and empowering. By tracking your spending, you'll get a clear understanding of where your money is going and be able to make smart decisions about how to use it.

So, how do you create a budget? Start by listing all your income sources and your monthly expenses, including things like rent/mortgage, utilities, groceries, entertainment, and so on. Then, subtract your expenses from your income to see if you're spending more than you're making. If you are, it's time to make some cuts.

Once you have your budget in place, stick to it! This means avoiding impulse purchases and thinking twice before making any big-ticket purchases. And don't forget to regularly track your spending to make sure you're staying on track.

But what about unexpected expenses? Life happens, and sometimes you'll have to spend money on things you weren't planning for. That's why it's a good idea to have an emergency fund in place. Aim to save up three to six months' worth of living expenses so you'll have a cushion in case of a financial emergency.

Now, I know budgeting can seem daunting, but once you get the hang of it, you'll wonder how you ever lived without a budget. With the power of a budget on your side, you'll be able to take control of your finances and live life on your own terms. So, let's get started!

Dining in Style: Saving Money on Food

Y'all ready for some food for thought? Because in this chapter, we're gonna talk about how to save big bucks on the grub you love.

Let's address the elephant in the room: eating out is expensive. Whether it's grabbing a quick bite on the go or treating yourself to a fancy dinner, dining out can put a serious dent in your budget. But that doesn't mean you have to give up your love for good food.

Enter meal planning. This is your secret weapon to saving money on food. By planning your meals in advance, you'll know exactly what you need to buy at the grocery store and avoid impulse purchases. Plus, you can take advantage of sales and stock up on ingredients when they're on sale.

Another tip for saving money on food is to cook at home. Not only will you save money, but you'll also have more control over what you're eating. So fire up that stove, and get ready to cook up a storm. And if you're feeling fancy, why not try your hand at gourmet cooking? With a little bit of creativity, you can turn simple ingredients into a culinary masterpiece.

But what about when you do want to eat out? No problem! Just be smart about it. Look for restaurant deals and coupons, and consider splitting a meal with a friend to save money. And if you're feeling particularly frugal, why not pack a picnic and enjoy a meal in the park?

Finally, don't forget about leftovers! They're your friend. By storing leftovers in the fridge or freezer, you'll have a delicious meal ready to go whenever you need it.

So there you have it, folks. With a little bit of planning and some smart choices, you can save money on food and still enjoy the dining experience. So, let's raise a fork to frugal living and dig in!

Thrifty Shopping: Finding the Best Deals

Listen up, shoppers! If you're looking to save some dough, you need to learn the art of thrifty shopping. And let me tell you, being a savvy shopper is a real game-changer.

First things first, know what you need before you hit the stores. Make a list of what you need and stick to it. This will help you avoid impulse purchases and ensure that you're getting the best deals.

Next, do your research. Before you buy anything, check online for coupons or promo codes. And don't forget to compare prices at different stores to make sure you're getting the best deal.

Another tip for thrifty shopping is to buy in bulk. This is especially true for items like non-perishable food and toiletries that you use regularly. Just make sure to store the items properly to ensure they don't go bad.

But what about big-ticket items? Don't worry, there are ways to save money on those too. Consider buying used or refurbished items, or wait for sales and clearance events to get the best deals.

Finally, don't be afraid to haggle. If you're buying something from a private seller or at a market, see if you can negotiate the price. You'll be surprised at how often people are willing to make a deal.

So there you have it, folks. With a little bit of research and smart shopping habits, you can save big bucks on your purchases. So, let's hit the stores and start shopping like a pro!

Frugal Fashion: Dressing for Less

Fashion lovers, it's time to listen up! Because in this chapter, we're gonna talk about how to look fabulous without breaking the bank.

First, invest in quality basics. A well-made pair of jeans, a classic white t-shirt, and a versatile black dress will form the foundation of your wardrobe and can be dressed up or down for any occasion. And the best part? They'll last you for years, saving you money in the long run.

Next, shop at second-hand stores. You'd be surprised at the gems you can find at thrift stores, consignment shops, and online marketplaces. Just make sure to check for signs of wear and tear before you buy.

And what about keeping up with the latest trends? Don't worry, there are ways to stay on trend without spending a fortune. Look for fast fashion brands that offer cheaper versions of the latest styles, or try to incorporate trendier pieces into your existing wardrobe.

Another tip for frugal fashion is to accessorize. A simple outfit can be transformed with the right accessories, so don't be afraid to experiment with jewelry, hats, and bags.

Finally, don't be afraid to get creative. With a little bit of imagination, you can turn old clothes into new outfits or even make your own clothes. Who knows, you might just discover a new hobby!

With a little bit of creativity and smart shopping habits, you can have a fabulous wardrobe without breaking the bank. So, let's get dressed and hit the town in style!

Grooming on a Budget: Taking Care of Your Appearance

Attention, beauty buffs! It's time to talk about taking care of your appearance without breaking the bank.

Invest in quality skincare products. A good skincare routine can go a long way in keeping your skin looking its best. And the best part? You don't have to spend a fortune to get quality products. Look for brands that offer high-quality products at affordable prices, or make your own skincare products using ingredients you already have at home.

Be smart about your haircare. Instead of going to a salon every time you need a trim, consider getting your hair cut at a cosmetology school. Not only will you save money, but you'll also be helping out a student in need of practice.

And what about makeup? Instead of splurging on expensive makeup, look for affordable alternatives. There are plenty of drugstore brands that offer high-quality products at a fraction of the cost. And remember, less is often more when it comes to makeup.

Another tip for grooming on a budget is to focus on good habits. Eating a balanced diet, staying hydrated, and getting enough sleep can go a long way in keeping you looking and feeling your best.

Finally, don't be afraid to get creative. With a little bit of imagination, you can create your own spa day at home, complete with DIY facials, manicures, and massages.

So there you have it, folks. With a little bit of smart shopping and good habits, you can take care of your appearance. So, let's pamper ourselves and look and feel our best!

Home Sweet Home: Cutting Costs on Housing

Listen up, homebodies! This chapter is all about making your house a home without breaking the bank.

Get creative with your living space. Instead of buying new furniture, consider upcycling or repurposing old pieces. You'd be surprised at what a fresh coat of paint or a new set of cushions can do for a tired piece of furniture.

Next, be energy-efficient. Simple changes, like using LED light bulbs, turning off lights when you leave a room, and unplugging electronics when they're not in use, can make a big difference in your energy bills.

And what about utility bills? Try to use water, gas, and electricity wisely. This can mean taking shorter showers, washing clothes in cold water, and using a clothesline instead of a dryer.

Another tip for cutting costs on housing is to shop around for the best deals on insurance, rent, and mortgage payments. Don't be afraid to negotiate and compare prices to get the best deal.

Finally, get involved in your community. Participating in local events, meeting your neighbors, and volunteering can not only help you save money, but also create a sense of community and belonging.

With a little bit of creativity and smart shopping habits, you can make your house a home without breaking the bank. Let's get cozy and enjoy the comforts of home!

Living with Less: The Benefits of Minimalism

Attention, clutter-haters! This chapter is all about embracing the minimalist lifestyle.

Let's talk about the benefits of living with less. When you have fewer possessions, you have less to clean, maintain, and organize. This can free up time and energy to focus on the things that truly matter, like relationships and personal growth.

Minimalism can also have a positive impact on your finances. By reducing your consumption, you can save money and reduce your environmental impact. Plus, the less you own, the less you have to worry about losing or damaging.

Next, let's talk about how to embrace minimalism. Start by decluttering your living space. Get rid of anything you don't use, need, or love. This can mean selling, donating, or recycling items you no longer need.

And what about shopping? Try to buy only what you need and avoid impulse purchases. Consider buying second-hand items when possible, as this can help you save money and reduce your environmental impact.

Another tip for living with less is to focus on experiences rather than possessions. Instead of buying things, consider going on a trip, trying a new restaurant, or taking a class.

Finally, remember that minimalism is a journey, not a destination. Embracing the minimalist lifestyle is about finding balance and creating a life that is meaningful and fulfilling.

With a little bit of decluttering and smart shopping habits, you can embrace the minimalist lifestyle and enjoy the benefits of living with less. So, let's simplify and live life to the fullest!

Green Living: Saving Money and the Environment

Attention, eco-warriors! This chapter is all about living a greener, more sustainable life.

Let's talk about the benefits of green living. Not only can it help protect the environment, but it can also save you money. Simple changes, like reducing your energy consumption and waste, can have a big impact on your finances and the planet.

Next, let's talk about how to live a greener life. Start by reducing your energy consumption. This can mean using energy-efficient appliances, turning off lights when you leave a room, and using a clothesline instead of a dryer.

And what about waste? Try to reduce, reuse, and recycle as much as possible. This can mean composting food waste, using reusable bags, and buying products with minimal packaging.

Another tip for green living is to support sustainable products and practices. Consider buying locally-sourced and organic food, using natural cleaning products, and supporting companies that are environmentally responsible.

Finally, remember that green living is a journey, not a destination. Embracing a greener lifestyle is about making small changes that add up to a big impact.

There you have it, folks. With a little bit of energy conservation and smart shopping habits, you can live a greener, more sustainable life. So, let's protect the planet and enjoy the benefits of green living!

Transportation: Getting Around Without Breaking the Bank

Listen up, all you road warriors and transit riders! This chapter is all about how to save money on transportation.

First, let's talk about the different transportation options available. Depending on where you live, you may have access to public transportation, bikes, or cars. Each of these options has its own costs and benefits, so it's important to weigh them carefully when making a decision.

If you live in an area with good public transportation, consider taking advantage of it. Not only can it save you money on gas, maintenance, and insurance, but it can also help reduce your carbon footprint. Plus, you can catch up on your reading or take a nap on your daily commute!

If public transportation isn't an option, consider carpooling or using a bike to get around. Carpooling can save you money on gas and reduce your carbon footprint, while biking is a great way to get exercise and save money on transportation costs.

When it comes to buying a car, consider purchasing a used car instead of a new one. Not only can this save you thousands of dollars, but it can also reduce your carbon footprint by avoiding the energy and resources needed to produce a new car.

Finally, consider your driving habits. Simple changes, like reducing your speed and avoiding rapid acceleration, can help you save money on gas and reduce your carbon footprint.

So, whether you're taking public transportation, biking, or driving, there are many ways to save money on transportation costs. The key is to find the option that works best for you and your budget!

Technology: Keeping Up with the Latest without Breaking the Bank

Alright tech lovers, this chapter is for you! We know how hard it is to resist the latest and greatest gadgets, but with a little bit of frugal know-how, you can have your tech and save money too.

First, consider purchasing refurbished or pre-owned technology instead of brand new. These products have often been gently used and come at a fraction of the cost of a brand new device. Just make sure to do your research and buy from a reputable seller.

Another option is to wait until the latest and greatest has been on the market for a while. Often times, prices will drop as newer models are introduced, so you can get the latest technology without paying full price.

When it comes to cell phone plans, consider switching to a more cost-effective option, like a prepaid or a budget carrier. You can also save money by reducing your data usage, choosing a phone with a longer battery life, and avoiding accidental overages.

Finally, don't forget about free alternatives to expensive software and apps. Many free alternatives offer the same functionality as their paid counterparts, so do your research and find the option that works best for you.

So there you have it! By following these tips, you can keep up with the latest technology without breaking the bank. Get ready to upgrade your tech and upgrade your savings!

Entertainment: Having Fun without Spending a Fortune

We all need a little bit of fun in our lives, but that doesn't mean we need to break the bank to do it. So buckle up, because we're about to take you on a frugal ride to some of the most entertaining experiences you'll ever have!

First and foremost, take advantage of the great outdoors. Go for a hike, have a picnic, or simply take a walk. Not only is it free, but it's also great for your health and well-being.

If you're in the mood for some indoor entertainment, consider renting a movie or a TV series instead of going to the theaters. You can also explore free or low-cost options like library book clubs, museum visits, or local theater performances.

For those who enjoy live entertainment, check out free community events or look for discounts on tickets. You can also attend smaller shows at local venues or bars, which are often more affordable than big concerts or sporting events.

And don't forget about the world of video games! Instead of buying new games all the time, try trading or swapping games with friends, renting games from a library, or downloading free or low-cost games from the internet.

With a little bit of creativity and some good old-fashioned elbow grease, you can have a whole lot of fun without spending a fortune. Happy entertaining!

Health and Wellness: Staying Fit on a Budget

Listen up, folks, because this is one chapter you don't want to miss. We all know that taking care of our health and wellness is important, but it doesn't have to cost a fortune. In fact, you can get fit and feel fantastic without breaking the bank!

Exercise doesn't have to mean hitting the gym. Take a walk, go for a run, or try a yoga class in your local park. You can also explore online workout videos or use apps that offer free or low-cost workout routines.

If you prefer group fitness, look for community centers, YMCAs, or local parks that offer free or low-cost classes. And don't be afraid to try new things like rock climbing, martial arts, or dance classes.

Eating healthy can also be a frugal endeavor. Plan your meals, buy in bulk, and make use of seasonal produce to save money. Try cooking at home instead of eating out, and you'll be surprised at how much money you can save. And don't forget about taking care of your mental health! Practice mindfulness, meditation, or therapy to help manage stress and anxiety. You can also look for low-cost or free support groups or online resources.

Staying healthy and fit doesn't have to cost a fortune. With a little bit of effort and creativity, you can live your best life without breaking the bank. Now go out there and take care of yourself!

Traveling Cheap: Exploring the World on a Tight Budget

Buckle up, folks, because we're about to go on a wild ride! The world is a big, beautiful place, and you don't need a lot of money to see it. In fact, with a little bit of planning and creativity, you can travel the world on a tight budget!

First things first, be flexible with your travel dates. Booking your trip during the off-season or on weekdays can save you big bucks on flights and accommodations. And when it comes to lodging your stay, consider alternative options like hostels, homestays, or vacation rentals.

Food is another big expense when traveling, but with a little bit of research, you can find local gems that won't break the bank. Try street food, local markets, or even grocery stores to save money on meals.

When it comes to sightseeing, opt for free or low-cost options like parks, museums, or historical landmarks. You can also save money by researching and purchasing tickets in advance or taking advantage of free walking tours.

And finally, don't forget about transportation! Take advantage of public transportation, rent a bike, or consider a road trip to save money and see more of the local area.

With a little bit of planning and creativity, you can travel the world on a tight budget. So pack your bags and get ready for an adventure! The world is yours to explore, and there's no better time to do it than now. Happy travels!

Romance on a Budget: Date Night Ideas

Ladies and gentlemen, it's time to turn up the heat and show your significant other a good time, all without breaking the bank! Believe it or not, you don't need a lot of money to have a romantic night out.

Start by setting the mood with a candlelit dinner at home. Cook a meal together or order in from your favorite restaurant, and don't forget to pop open a bottle of wine. Plus, who says you can't wear your fancy clothes at home? Dress up and enjoy a night in!

If you're looking to get out of the house, take a stroll through your local park or beach. Bring a picnic and enjoy the beautiful scenery, or watch the stars while cuddled up together.

Take advantage of free events in your city, like concerts in the park, festivals, or street fairs. These events are a great way to spend time together and experience new things.

Get creative and try a DIY project together, like painting pottery or creating your own candles. And if you're feeling adventurous, take a dance class together or sign up for a cooking class.

Don't forget about the little gestures that can make a big impact. Write love letters to each other, take a bubble bath together, or simply spend the evening cuddled up on the couch watching your favorite movie.

Whether you're staying in or going out, there are plenty of ways to have a romantic night without spending a fortune. Get out there and show your significant other a good time!

Gift Giving: Showing Your Love Without Spending a Lot

When it comes to gift giving, it's often said that it's the thought that counts. And we couldn't agree more! The best gifts come from the heart and don't have to break the bank.

Gift giving is an opportunity to show your loved ones how much you care, but it can also be a source of stress and financial strain, especially during the holiday season. If you're looking to cut costs without sacrificing quality or sentiment, we've got some great frugal gift-giving tips for you!

1. DIY gifts: Nothing says "I love you" like a handmade gift. Get creative and make something personal, like a scrapbook or a photo frame. You can use materials you already have around the house, and the recipient will appreciate the time and effort you put into it.
2. Experiences over things: Give the gift of memories! Plan a day trip or a fun activity, like hiking or cooking together. This type of gift is great for those who have everything, and you'll both have a great time making new memories.
3. Give from the heart: If you're on a tight budget, don't be afraid to be honest about it. You can still give a heartfelt gift, like a love letter or a thoughtful note. These gifts may be small, but they pack a big punch.
4. Use coupons and discounts: If you do want to give a physical gift, use coupons and discounts to make it

more affordable. You can often find great deals on items you were already planning to purchase.

5. Regift with care: Regifting can be a great way to save money, but it's important to do it thoughtfully. Make sure the item you're regifting is something the recipient will actually want, and avoid giving gifts that have sentimental value to you.

In conclusion, gift giving doesn't have to break the bank. By being creative, thoughtful, and using discounts, you can show your love without going into debt. So next time you're looking to give a gift, remember, it's the thought that counts!

Holidays: Celebrating in Style Without Breaking the Bank

It's the most wonderful time of the year... or so the song goes. But let's be real, the holidays can also be the most expensive time of the year. Between gift buying, travel, and all the special meals, it can feel like you're constantly dipping into your wallet. But don't worry, my frugal friends, I've got your back. With a little creativity and a pinch of holiday spirit, you can celebrate in style without breaking the bank.

First things first, let's talk gifts. One of the biggest expenses during the holidays is buying presents for loved ones. Instead of going all-out on expensive gifts, consider homemade or thoughtful gestures. Baked goods, handmade ornaments, or a personalized photo album are just a few ideas that can show your love without putting a dent in your bank account. Another option is to participate in a gift exchange, where everyone brings one gift and you pick out of a hat to see who you get to buy for. This helps keep the spending in check and is a fun way to get involved with the gifting aspect of the holidays.

When it comes to travel, try to plan ahead and book flights, trains, or buses in advance. The earlier you book, the cheaper the tickets tend to be. Also, consider alternative options like staying with family or friends instead of booking a hotel. And if you do have to stay in a hotel, look for deals and discounts on websites.

Food is another big part of the holidays, and it's easy to go overboard on fancy meals and treats. But there's no need to spend a fortune to have a delicious meal. Try potluck-style gatherings where everyone brings a dish to share. Or, host a holiday brunch instead of a dinner, since brunch foods tend to be less expensive than dinner foods. And don't forget about the leftovers! A turkey sandwich the day after Thanksgiving can be just as satisfying as a fancy feast.

Finally, don't forget to have fun and enjoy the holiday spirit. Decorations and lights are a big part of the holidays, but you don't have to buy all new decorations every year. Consider making your own ornaments or buying second-hand decorations at a holiday market. And if you're feeling adventurous, try caroling or ice skating for free entertainment.

In conclusion, the holidays don't have to be a financial burden. With a little creativity and a focus on the true meaning of the season, you can celebrate in style without breaking the bank. And who knows, you might even have more fun and make better memories doing it!

Education: Investing in Yourself on a Budget

Alright folks, it's time to talk about one of the most important investments you'll ever make: education. Whether you're looking to learn a new skill, advance in your career, or just satisfy your curiosity, there's no denying that education is a valuable commodity.

The good news is, you don't have to break the bank to invest in your education. In fact, there are plenty of ways to continue learning without spending a fortune. Let's dive into some of the most cost-effective ways to keep your brain sharp.

1. Online Courses: With the rise of the internet, there's never been a better time to learn online. From massive open online courses to more specialized programs, there's a wealth of educational resources at your fingertips. And the best part? Many of these courses are free or very low-cost.
2. Public Libraries: Don't underestimate the power of your local library. Not only do they have a wealth of books and resources for you to borrow, but many libraries also offer free classes and workshops on a variety of topics.
3. Community Colleges: Community colleges are a great option for those who want to further their education without going into debt. With lower tuition costs and smaller class sizes, community colleges provide a more affordable alternative to traditional four-year universities.

4. Professional Workshops and Conferences: If you're looking to advance in your career, attending professional workshops and conferences can be a great way to learn new skills and network with like-minded individuals. Just be sure to shop around for the best deals, as these events can sometimes be pricey.
5. Self-Study: Finally, don't forget the power of self-study. Whether you're learning a new language, reading books on a topic you're passionate about, or taking online tutorials, there are plenty of ways to educate yourself without spending a dime.

So there you have it folks, a few cost-effective ways to invest in your education. Whether you're looking to pick up a new skill or just satisfy your curiosity, there's no excuse not to continue learning. Happy studying!

Starting a Business: Entrepreneurship on a Budget

Starting a business can be an exciting and fulfilling experience, but it can also be an expensive one. From marketing to product development, there are many expenses that come with launching a new venture. But fear not, my frugal friends! With a little creativity and a lot of smart planning, you can start a business without breaking the bank.

First things first, you've got to have an idea. Whether it's a product or a service, you need to figure out what you're passionate about and what you're good at. Take a look at your skills, interests, and the market demand, and brainstorm a list of potential business ideas. You can even start small by offering your services as a freelancer or selling your products online.

Once you have a solid idea, it's time to start planning. Set your goals, create a business plan, and map out a budget. This will help you stay organized and focused, and it'll give you an idea of the costs involved. Don't forget to factor in all of the expenses, including marketing, web development, and equipment.

When it comes to marketing, there are many ways to get the word out without spending a fortune. Utilize social media, create a website, and reach out to your network for help spreading the word. You can also participate in local events, offer discounts to your friends and family, and leverage word-of-mouth marketing.

When it comes to product development, you can save money by using low-cost materials, outsourcing work to freelancers, or using digital tools and software. You can also test your product with a small group of customers before launching it to the wider market. This will help you refine your product and make it the best it can be before investing more money into it.

Starting a business on a budget is all about being creative and resourceful. With the right mindset and a little bit of determination, you can turn your entrepreneurial dreams into a reality. So go ahead, take the leap, and start that business today! You'll be amazed at what you can achieve with a little bit of frugal ingenuity.

Investing: Growing Your Money

Let's talk about investing! It's one of those words that can make even the bravest of us break into a sweat, but don't worry, I promise we'll take it slow. The key to investing is to remember that it's all about the long game. You're not going to become a millionaire overnight, but with a little patience and smart decisions, you can watch your money grow over time.

So, what are your options? Well, there's stocks, bonds, mutual funds, and even real estate. But the best part? You don't have to break the bank to start investing. In fact, you can start with just a few bucks and build from there.

Let's start with stocks. They can be a bit intimidating, but the idea is simple: you're buying a piece of a company. The hope is that the company does well, the stock goes up in value, and you make a profit when you sell. The key is to do your research and pick companies that have a strong track record and a bright future ahead. And remember, don't put all your eggs in one basket! Diversification is key when it comes to investing in stocks.

Next up, we've got bonds. They're a little different from stocks in that they're more like a loan. When you buy a bond, you're lending money to the company or government that issued it. In return, they promise to pay you back with interest. It's a more stable option than stocks, but the returns are generally lower.

Mutual funds are a great option for those who want a little bit of both. They're a collection of stocks and bonds, managed by a professional. The idea is that the professional will make smart investment decisions for you, so you don't have to do all the heavy lifting. Plus, because you're pooling your money with other investors, you can get exposure to a wider range of investments.

Finally, let's talk about real estate. It's not for everyone, but it can be a great investment if you do it right. The idea is to buy a property, rent it out, and let the rent money cover the mortgage and any expenses. Over time, the property will appreciate in value, and you can sell it for a profit. Just be prepared for a lot of work and responsibility, as you'll be a landlord and have to take care of the property and deal with tenants.

In conclusion, investing doesn't have to be scary or expensive. With a little research and a long-term mindset, you can start growing your money and building wealth today. Just remember, the key is to be patient and make smart decisions. Happy investing!

Insurance: Protecting Your Finances

Hey there, savvy savers! In this chapter, we're going to talk about one of the most important aspects of frugal living – insurance. It's not the most thrilling topic, but let's be real, accidents happen and you don't want to be caught off guard. That's why it's essential to protect your finances with the right insurance policies.

First things first, what do you need insurance for? Well, let's think about it. You have your car, your home, your health, and your life to consider. And if anything were to happen to any of these, you don't want to be stuck paying a massive bill out of pocket. So, it's a smart move to have insurance in place to cover these events.

Now, you might be thinking, "But insurance is so expensive!" And while it's true that insurance can be pricey, the peace of mind and protection it provides is well worth the cost. Plus, there are ways to keep your insurance costs down.

For example, when shopping for insurance, make sure to compare quotes from different providers. Don't just go with the first company you come across – do your research and find the best deal for you. Also, consider raising your deductibles. This means you'll have to pay more out of pocket if something happens, but it'll lower your monthly insurance premiums.

Another way to save on insurance is to bundle your policies. Many insurance companies offer discounts if you have multiple policies with them, such as car and home insurance. So, consider combining your policies to save some moolah.

And lastly, make sure you have the right coverage. Don't skimp on coverage just to save a few bucks. It's important to have enough coverage to protect your finances in the case of an emergency. So, take the time to review your policies and make sure you have the coverage you need.

In conclusion, insurance is a crucial part of frugal living. It's important to protect your finances and have peace of mind knowing you're covered if something were to happen. So, make sure you have the right policies in place and shop around for the best deal. Happy saving!

Estate Planning: Preparing for the Future

Ah, the future. It's a scary place full of uncertainty and wondering what's going to happen. But don't worry, I'm here to tell you about estate planning, the key to unlocking a stress-free future!

First off, let's define what estate planning is. Estate planning is the process of creating a plan for your assets and property after you pass away. This includes things like your house, money, stocks, and personal belongings. It's like a roadmap for your future, so that your loved ones know what to do with your assets once you're gone.

Now, you may be thinking, "I'm young, I don't need to worry about that stuff yet." But the truth is, it's never too early to start thinking about estate planning. The earlier you start, the more time you have to make informed decisions and to ensure that your wishes are fulfilled.

One of the first things to consider when estate planning is your will. A will is a legal document that outlines who you want to inherit your assets and property after you pass away. It's important to have a will in place, as it ensures that your assets are distributed according to your wishes, instead of being left to the laws of the state.

Another important aspect of estate planning is creating a trust. A trust is a legal arrangement where a trustee holds and manages assets for the benefit of someone else, known as the beneficiary. Trusts are a great way to protect your assets and pass them on to your loved ones without going through probate court.

It's also important to think about your future healthcare needs and wishes. You can do this by creating a living will or a healthcare power of attorney. A living will outlines your wishes for medical treatment in the event that you are unable to make decisions for yourself, and a healthcare power of attorney gives someone else the authority to make decisions on your behalf.

Lastly, it's important to have life insurance. Life insurance provides financial security for your loved ones in the event of your unexpected passing. It's a small price to pay for peace of mind knowing that your loved ones will be taken care of.

In conclusion, estate planning is a critical aspect of financial planning that should not be overlooked. It's never too early to start thinking about your future, and estate planning can help you ensure that your assets are distributed according to your wishes. So, start planning today and ensure a stress-free tomorrow!

Retirement - Planning for Your Golden Years

Alright folks, it's time to talk about the elephant in the room - retirement. I know, I know, it may seem like a long ways off but trust me, the earlier you start planning for it, the better. Because let's be real, nobody wants to be working until they drop dead, right?

So, what is retirement exactly? It's the time in your life when you stop working, put your feet up, and start living off the fruits of your labor. And the key to making this dream a reality is to start planning for it, like, yesterday!

First, let's talk about your goals. What kind of life do you want in retirement? Do you want to travel the world, take up a new hobby, or just relax at home? Knowing what you want will help you plan how much money you'll need to have saved up by the time you retire.

Next, let's talk about Social Security. It's a government-run program that provides a monthly income to eligible retirees. But, it's important to remember that Social Security is not meant to be your only source of retirement income, so don't rely on it too heavily.

Now, let's talk about retirement savings. The earlier you start saving for retirement, the more time your money has to grow, and the less you'll have to save each month.

But what if you're already in your golden years and haven't started planning for retirement yet? Don't worry, it's never too late to start. Consider downsizing your home, working part-time, or even starting a small business. The key is to start taking action, no matter how small, towards your retirement goals.

In conclusion, planning for retirement is one of the most important things you can do for your financial future. It's never too early or too late to start, and by taking control of your finances, you'll be able to enjoy your golden years with peace of mind. So, don't wait any longer, start planning for your retirement today!

Remember, retirement may seem like a distant dream but with a little planning and a lot of saving, you can make it a reality. And who knows, you might just find yourself sipping margaritas on a beach in Mexico, living the retirement dream.

Debt Management: Paying Off Your Debts and Living Like a Boss

Welcome to the chapter on debt management! If you're reading this, chances are you're up to your ears in debt and feeling like you're drowning in a sea of numbers. Don't worry, you're not alone, and there is hope for you yet! In this chapter, we'll be covering the basics of debt management and giving you some solid tips and tricks for paying off your debts and living like a boss.

First, let's talk about what debt is and why it's important to manage it. Debt is simply an amount of money that you owe to someone else. It can come in many forms, such as credit card debt, student loan debt, mortgage debt, and more. While debt can be a useful tool for helping us achieve our financial goals, it can also be a dangerous trap if we don't keep it under control.

The first step in managing your debt is to get a handle on exactly how much you owe. Gather up all your credit card statements, loan statements, and any other bills that you have that show the amount you owe. Add up all the debts you owe and you'll have a good idea of the total amount of debt you're carrying.

Next, you need to create a budget. A budget is simply a plan for how you're going to use your money. It helps you keep track of your spending and make sure you're using your money in a way that's in line with your goals. When creating your budget, make sure to include a line item for debt repayment. This will help you prioritize paying off your debts and keep you on track.

Once you've created your budget, it's time to start attacking your debts one by one. The most popular method for paying off debt is the debt snowball method. This method involves paying off your smallest debt first, then using the money you were using to pay that debt to pay off the next smallest debt, and so on. This method works because it gives you quick wins and helps build momentum, which can be very motivational.

Another method for paying off debt is the debt avalanche method. This method involves paying off your debt with the highest interest rate first. This method is best for those who have a lot of high-interest debt and want to pay it off as quickly as possible.

Regardless of which method you choose, make sure to stick to your budget and keep paying off your debts each month. You'll be surprised at how quickly your debts will start to disappear!

So, what are you waiting for? Get started on your debt management journey today! With some discipline and a solid plan, you'll be debt-free in no time and living like a boss!

Credit Management: Building and Maintaining Good Credit

Ah, the almighty credit score. It can make or break your financial future, and yet, most of us don't even know what it is until it's too late. But fear not, my friends, because building and maintaining good credit is not as complicated as it may seem. In fact, it's actually quite simple when you know the tricks of the trade. So, grab a cup of coffee (or tea, or whatever your preferred beverage is), and let's dive in!

First, what is credit? Simply put, credit is the ability to borrow money from a lender. This can include loans, credit cards, and mortgages. Your credit score is a numerical representation of your creditworthiness and is calculated based on a number of factors, including payment history, credit utilization, length of credit history, types of credit, and new credit. A good credit score can open doors for you, from getting approved for a loan to landing your dream job (yes, some employers check your credit score).

Now that you know what credit is, let's talk about how to build and maintain good credit.

1. Payment history: This is the most important factor in determining your credit score. Simply put, make all your payments on time and in full. Late payments and defaults can have a huge impact on your score, so set up automatic payments or reminders if you need to.

2. Credit utilization: This refers to the amount of credit you're using compared to the amount you have available. The general rule of thumb is to keep your utilization below 30% of your available credit. So, if you have a credit card with a limit of $10,000, try to keep your balance below $3,000.
3. Length of credit history: The longer you have credit, the better it is for your score. This shows lenders that you're responsible with credit and have a long-term track record of paying on time.
4. Types of credit: Having a mix of different types of credit (such as a credit card, a loan, and a mortgage) can also improve your score. This shows that you're able to manage different types of credit responsibly.
5. New credit: Every time you apply for credit, it shows up as a "hard inquiry" on your credit report. Too many hard inquiries in a short period of time can lower your score, so try to limit the number of new credit applications.

Now that you know the key factors that determine your credit score, let's talk about some tips for maintaining good credit.

1. Check your credit report regularly: It's important to check your credit report regularly to make sure there are no errors.
2. Be aware of fraud: Keep an eye out for fraud and report it immediately if you suspect anything. Identity theft can have a major impact on your credit score, so it's important to stay vigilant.
3. Don't close old credit accounts: Closing old credit accounts can shorten your credit history, which can lower your score. Instead, try to keep them open and use them occasionally to keep them active.

4. Pay off debt: The amount of debt you have can also impact your credit score, so try to pay off as much debt as possible. This will also improve your credit utilization and reduce your debt-to-income ratio, which is another factor that lenders look at.
5. Be patient: Building good credit takes time. It's important to be patient and not get discouraged if you don't see immediate results. Keep making timely payments, keeping your credit utilization low, and checking your credit report regularly. With time and dedication, you'll be able to build and maintain good credit.

Credit Management is an important aspect of your financial life. By understanding how credit works, starting early, keeping your credit utilization low, making payments on time, not closing credit accounts, checking your credit report regularly, and being patient, you can establish a solid credit history that will benefit you in the long run. Remember, good credit takes time and effort, but the payoff is well worth it.

Saving for Emergencies - Preparing for the Unexpected

Let's be real, life can be a real wild card sometimes. You never know when you might lose your job, get hit with an unexpected medical bill, or have your car break down at the worst possible moment. That's why it's important to have a plan in place to weather these financial storms. And that, my friends, is what we call an emergency fund.

An emergency fund is simply a stash of cash that you set aside specifically for unexpected expenses. Think of it as a cushion for life's curveballs. The goal is to have enough money saved up so that you can cover three to six months' worth of living expenses in case of a job loss or other financial emergency.

Now, I know what you might be thinking: "That sounds great in theory, but where am I supposed to find the money to save?" Don't worry, I've got you covered. You can start small and gradually increase your contributions over time. Here are a few tips to get you started:

1. Start with a goal: Determine how much you want to save and when you want to reach your goal. This will give you a roadmap to follow and help you stay motivated.
2. Make it automatic: Set up an automatic transfer from your checking account to a separate savings account for your emergency fund. This way, you'll be consistently saving a little bit each month without even thinking about it.

3. Trim your expenses: Take a look at your monthly spending and see where you can cut back. Maybe you can skip that weekly latte or cancel that subscription you never use. Every little bit helps.
4. Pick up a side hustle: If you're feeling extra ambitious, you can always earn a little extra cash on the side to help boost your emergency fund. Try selling some of your unwanted items online, offering your services as a freelancer, or even doing odd jobs for friends and family.
5. Be patient: Building an emergency fund takes time, so be patient and stick with it. Remember, the goal is to have peace of mind knowing you have a safety net in case of an emergency.

Having an emergency fund in place is like having a financial safety net. It gives you peace of mind knowing that you're prepared for the unexpected. So, don't wait until it's too late - start building your emergency fund today!

Life is full of surprises, but with a little preparation, you can be ready for whatever comes your way. An emergency fund is the key to financial peace of mind, and with a little bit of discipline and a whole lot of determination, you can have one in place before you know it. Happy savings!

Bargain Hunting: Finding the Best Deals Online

It's time to sharpen those bargain hunting skills of yours! Let's talk about finding the best deals online and saving a boatload of cash in the process. Who doesn't love the thrill of scoring a killer deal? It's like finding a needle in a haystack, but way more satisfying.

First, sign up for email alerts from your favorite stores. This way, you'll be the first to know about sales and promotions. Make use of those birthday discounts, it's your special day after all! And don't forget to check for coupon codes before making a purchase. It's amazing how often a simple Google search can lead to big savings.

Next up, make friends with social media. Following your favorite brands on Facebook, Instagram, and Twitter can result in exclusive deals and early access to sales. And don't be afraid to reach out and ask for a discount if you see something you like. Many companies are willing to offer a deal to their social media followers.

It's also worth checking out websites for deals on everything from clothes and electronics to dining and travel.

And last but not least, be a smart shopper! Compare prices at different stores and websites before making a purchase. Don't fall for the trap of thinking the first price you see is the best one. Take the time to shop around and find the best deal for you.

In conclusion, with a little bit of effort and research, you can score some amazing deals and save a ton of money. So get to it, happy bargain hunting!

Couponing: Maximizing Your Savings

Coupons, coupons, coupons! We all love the sound of that word, don't we? Who doesn't love to save money on their purchases? And with couponing, you can do just that! In this chapter, we're going to explore the wonderful world of coupons and show you how to maximize your savings.

First things first, let's talk about the different types of coupons. You have your basic store coupons, which can be found in the weekly ad, at the store entrance, or in your email inbox. Then there's manufacturer coupons, which can be found in the Sunday newspaper, on product packaging, or on websites. Lastly, you have printable coupons, which you can find online and print at home.

Now that you know the types of coupons, let's get down to business. To start, you'll want to make a list of the items you need and the brands you prefer. Then, check the weekly ads and websites for available coupons. Don't be afraid to stack your coupons either! This means using a store coupon with a manufacturer coupon to maximize your savings.

Another way to maximize your savings is to keep an eye out for sales. If a product you need is on sale, use a coupon to make the deal even sweeter. This is called "price matching," and many stores will allow you to use a coupon on a sale item to get the best price.

One tip to keep in mind is to only buy what you need. Just because you have a coupon doesn't mean you have to buy it. And don't forget to compare prices to ensure you're getting the best deal.

When it comes to organizing your coupons, there are a few methods to choose from. You can keep them in a binder with baseball card holders, file them in a coupon organizer, or even just clip them and keep them in a designated spot in your purse. Find what works best for you and stick with it!

Lastly, never be afraid to ask if a store accepts coupons or if they have any available. You'd be surprised at how many stores have coupons readily available for customers who ask.

So, are you ready to start couponing? Get your coupons and your shopping list ready and let's go! With a little bit of effort, you'll be surprised at how much money you can save. Happy couponing!

Freelancing: Making Money on the Side - Because Who Doesn't Love a Little Extra Dough?

Alright, let's talk about one of the hottest trends in the work world today – freelancing. This gig-based way of working has taken the world by storm, and for good reason. It offers the freedom to work from anywhere, set your own hours, and choose the projects that you want to work on. And the best part? You can make some serious cash on the side!

So, what is freelancing exactly? It's pretty simple, really. Freelancing refers to working for yourself, either as a self-employed individual or as an independent contractor. You take on projects or assignments from clients and complete them on your own time. No boss, no 9-5 schedule, and no office politics – sounds like a dream come true, right?

And the good news doesn't stop there. Freelancing is accessible to just about anyone, regardless of your education or background. Whether you're a graphic designer, writer, web developer, or even a virtual assistant, there's likely a freelancing gig out there that's right up your alley.

But where do you start? The first step is to figure out what skills or services you have to offer. This could be anything from designing logos to writing blog posts to managing social media accounts. Next, you'll want to create a portfolio that showcases your work. This could be as simple as a website with examples of your past projects, or even a LinkedIn profile that highlights your skills and experience.

Once you've got your portfolio up and running, it's time to start finding clients. There are a number of websites out there that specialize in connecting freelancers with potential clients, such as Upwork, Freelancer, and Fiverr. Simply create a profile, list your skills and services, and start bidding on projects that interest you.

Of course, freelancing isn't just about making money on the side – it's also about building your brand and expanding your network. So, be sure to take the time to market yourself effectively and build relationships with clients. Offer great customer service, meet deadlines, and go above and beyond to ensure that your clients are happy with the work you provide.

And don't forget to set your rates! As a freelancer, you have the power to determine what you're worth, so make sure you're pricing yourself appropriately for the level of skill and experience you bring to the table.

So there you have it – a crash course in freelancing. If you're looking to make some extra cash and enjoy the freedom of working for yourself, it's definitely worth considering. And who knows – you may just end up turning your side hustle into a full-time gig.

So get out there, start bidding on those projects, and make some money! Just remember – freelancing is a marathon, not a sprint. Be patient, stay focused, and always strive to improve your skills and offer better services to your clients. Good luck!

Conclusion: The Joy of Frugal Living and Living Richly

And here we are, folks, at the grand finale of our frugal living journey. The road may have been long and bumpy, but I hope you've enjoyed it and learned a thing or two along the way. But before we part ways, let's take a moment to reflect on all the knowledge we've gained and how we can put it into practice.

First, let's remember that frugal living isn't about being cheap or depriving ourselves of the things we love. It's about living within our means, being mindful of our spending, and making the most out of every dollar. It's about finding joy in the simple things and not always having to chase after the latest and greatest.

So, how do we put this newfound wisdom into action? Start by setting realistic goals and priorities. Do you want to save more money, reduce your debt, or invest in your future? Whatever it is, write it down and make a plan to achieve it. Don't be afraid to seek the help of a financial advisor or consult online resources if you need to.

Next, be intentional with your spending. Keep track of your expenses and figure out where you can cut back. Look for ways to save money on everyday purchases and take advantage of deals and discounts. Remember, a little goes a long way, so don't be discouraged if progress is slow.

Another key component of frugal living is finding balance. It's okay to treat yourself from time to time, but do so in moderation. Look for free or low-cost activities to fill your free time, like hiking, reading, or volunteering. These experiences can be just as enriching as expensive ones, if not more.

Finally, embrace the spirit of frugal living by sharing your knowledge and experiences with others. Teach your children the value of a hard-earned dollar and encourage them to live frugally. Share recipes, tips, and tricks with friends and family. The more people that adopt this lifestyle, the more we can all benefit from it.

In conclusion, frugal living is a wonderful and fulfilling way of life that can enrich us in more ways than one. By living within our means and finding joy in the simple things, we can live richly and achieve financial stability. So, my friends, I leave you with this final piece of advice: live frugally, live richly, and live life to the fullest.

Well folks, we've come to the end of our frugal living journey together, and I hope you've found it as informative and entertaining as I have. If you're anything like me, you're now feeling confident and excited to put all the tips and tricks you've learned into practice.

But before you go, I want to give a big thank you for taking the time to read this guide. Your support means the world to me, and I'm grateful for every one of you.

And if you've enjoyed the ride, I'd be ever so grateful if you could leave a little love in the form of a positive review. It'll help others discover this guide, and let me know that all my hard work has paid off.

So, until next time folks, happy frugal living, and here's to living richly in every sense of the word!